Car Journey

Deborah Chancellor
Photography by Chris Fairclough

FRANKLIN WATTS
LONDON•SYDNEY

This edition 2005

Franklin Watts
338 Euston Road
London NW1 3BH

Franklin Watts Australia
Hachette Children's Books
Level 17/207 Kent Street
Sydney NSW 2000

ISBN-10: 0 7496 6111 9
ISBN-13: 978 0 7496 6111 3
Dewey Decimal Classification 912
A CIP record for this book is available from the British Library

Printed in Malaysia

Series editor: Sarah Peutrill
Series design: Peter Scoulding
Design: Hardlines
Photographs: Chris Fairclough
Consultant: Steve Watts

Map on page 13 'Crown Copyright Licence No. 100019031' Estate Publications
Map on page 20 courtesy of the National Trust

With thanks to the National Trust's Fountains Abbey & Studley Royal Estate
Also thanks to Kevin, Susie, Annabel and Peter

Contents

Starting Out

Distance travelled on this part of the route: 6.5 km. Total distance: 6.5 km.

Mum, Dad, Peter and Annabel live in Leeds, a **city** in the north of England. Their house is in an area called Holt Park, which is in the north-west of the city.

Today the family are going on a day trip.

*Leeds is in the **county** of Yorkshire.*

The family are going to visit Fountains Abbey, near Ripon.

Before they set off, Mum checks the **route** on a **road map**.

The family drive out of Holt Park, turning left onto a major road called the A660. They travel north, passing through a **village** called Bramhope.

They drive through Bramhope on the A660.

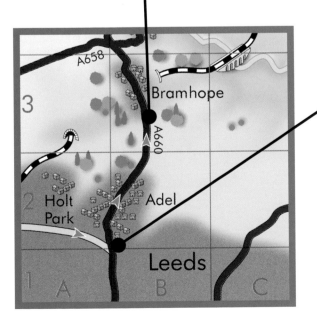

The family turn left here.

You can follow each stage of the family's journey on route maps like this one.

Into the Country

Distance travelled on this part of the route: 5.75 km. Total distance: 12.25 km.

Just beyond Bramhope, the family reach a **crossroads**. They turn right to join the A658. This road takes them down a hill and into the village of Pool.

The car's headlights are on because it is a dull, rainy morning.

The children spot the River Wharfe sign next to the bridge.

RIVER WHARFE

Just north of Pool, the family cross a bridge over the River Wharfe. They continue on to a small **town** called Huby. Peter spots a railway station as he looks out of the window

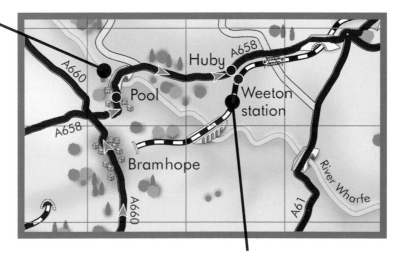

The family cross Pool Bridge here.

The children see this station from the road.

By the Railway

Distance travelled on this part of the route: 3.75 km. Total distance: 16 km.

As the family leave Huby, the children look for the railway line. They see a **level crossing** on their right.

The gates are down on the level crossing because a train is passing.

At a place called Nab Hill, the family drive over a bridge to cross the track.

The children spot this level crossing.

They turn left at this roundabout.

This is the bridge over the railway line.

Soon, they come to a **roundabout**, where they turn left, following the sign for Harrogate. The road they take is called the A61.

The North (A1)
York A 658 (A 59)

Harrogate
A 61

Leeds
A 61

Through the Town

Distance travelled on this part of the route: 7.25 km. Total distance: 23.25 km.

The family travel north towards Harrogate. They cross two bridges. The first goes over the railway line, and the second goes over the River Crimple.

The family drive straight through Harrogate. They pass a pretty park in the town centre. This park is called The Stray.

40

Welcome to HARROGATE please drive carefully

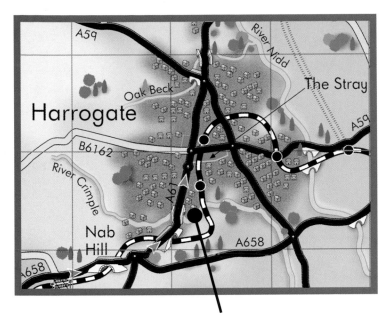

The River Crimple flows to the south of Harrogate.

The **street map** below shows Harrogate in greater detail. It is a large **scale** map. All the streets are named, and important features of the town are shown.

This map is covered with a grid, which helps people to find a particular street or place. For example East Park Road is in D5 – can you find it?

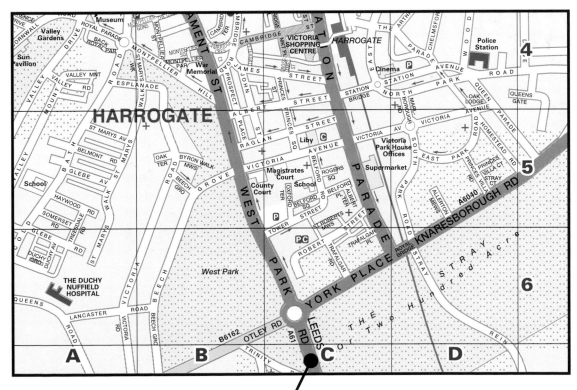

The family drive through Harrogate on the A61.

Over Bridges

The family leave Harrogate travelling north. They drive over a bridge, crossing a stream called Oak Beck. This stream flows into the River Nidd, to the east of the A61.

The family drive slowly though the village of Killinghall.

*The village sign is on an old **millstone**.*

Just north of Killinghall, the family drive over another bridge, this time over the River Nidd.

The A61 crosses the River Nidd here.

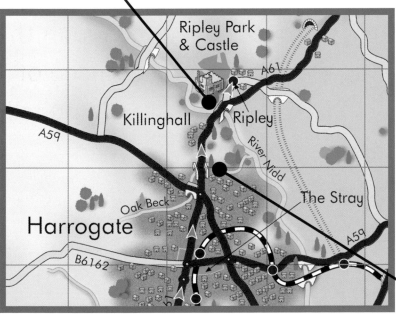

The family cross Oak Beck here.

Going North

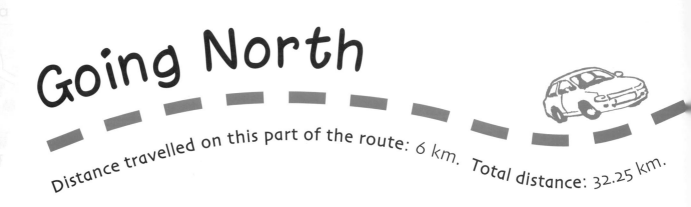

Distance travelled on this part of the route: 6 km. Total distance: 32.25 km.

Soon, Mum, Dad, Peter and Annabel approach the village of Ripley. The busy road they are on goes around the village. This means that heavy traffic is kept away from Ripley's quiet streets.

A smaller road leads into the village. The family take this country road and drive slowly through Ripley.

The A61 passes Ripley here.

This road leads into Ripley.

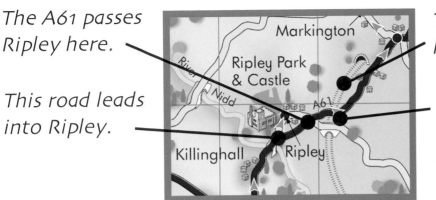

The disused railway line is here.

This is where the family stop for a snack. The road is very minor so it is not on the map.

The family rejoin the A61, then turn right into a quiet country road. They stop for a snack by a **disused railway line**. Then they return to the main road and continue on their way.

Disused railway lines like this are often popular with walkers.

Country Lanes

Distance travelled on this part of the route: 6.25 km. Total distance: 38.5 km.

When the family reach Wormald Green, it is time to leave the main road. They turn left into a country lane and drive to a village called Markington.

Cars use special passing places when roads are narrow like this.

At Markington they turn right and travel along more country lanes. These roads are so narrow, they are not given numbers or names on the map.

The tower is on a hilltop, so it is easy to see from the road.

Fountains Abbey Visitor Centre

The children look out for brown tourist signs. The family have to find their way by looking for these road signs and by following the map. **Landmarks** are also useful. Peter spots a tower out of the window. This helps Mum to work out where they are on the map.

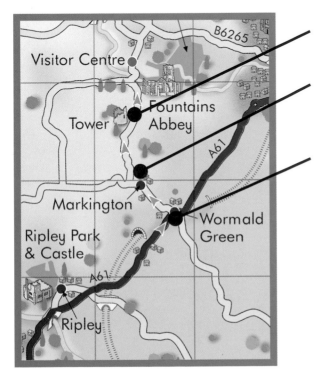

3 Peter sees this tower.

2 They turn right at Markington village.

1 This is where the family turn off the A61.

The family arrive at Fountains Abbey. Their journey has taken about an hour.

At Fountains Abbey

The family enter Fountains Abbey at the Visitor Centre.

They park the car and go inside the Visitor Centre. Here they look at a **plan** of the grounds. This helps them decide where they want to go.

This is a plan of the grounds.

The family have their picnic here.

They walk beside these lakes.

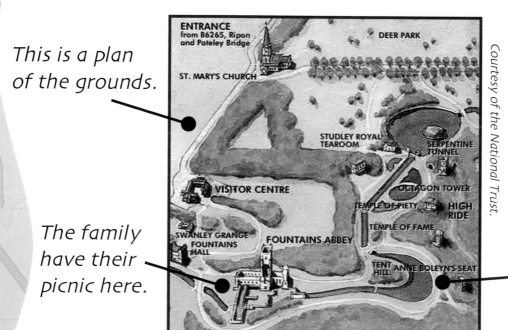

Courtesy of the National Trust.

At lunchtime, the family eat their picnic by the ruins of the abbey. Luckily for them, the clouds have disappeared and the sun is shining.

Can you see where the abbey is on the plan of the grounds?

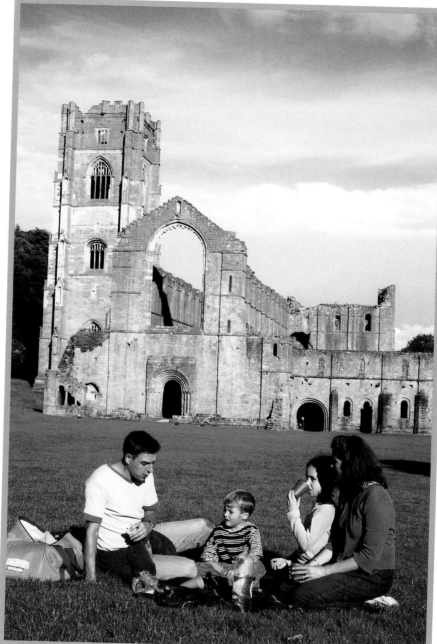

They spend the afternoon exploring the gardens and lakes of this beautiful place.

The Route Back

Distance travelled on this part of the route: 7.5 km. Total distance: 46 km.

At half past four, the family set off for home. They do not go back the same way, but go north until they reach a crossroads. At this **junction**, they turn right onto the B6265, following signs for Ripon.

The family drive through Ripon. In the city centre, they cross a bridge over the River Skell.

*The city's **cathedral** can be seen from the bridge.*

On the east side of the city, the family come to a roundabout. Here they follow signs for Harrogate, turning right onto the A61.

The family turn right at this crossroads.

The cathedral is here.

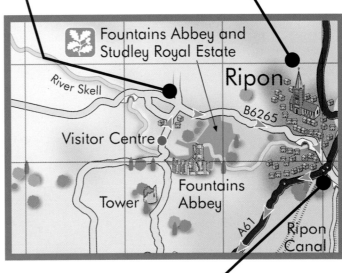

They join the A61 at this roundabout.

Getting Home

The family travel south from Ripon to Wormald Green. From this point, they are following exactly the same route as before, but going the other way.

*The children spot this **viaduct** on the way home. It carries the railway line over the River Wharfe.*

Now that they are going in the opposite **direction** the children spot different things out of the window.

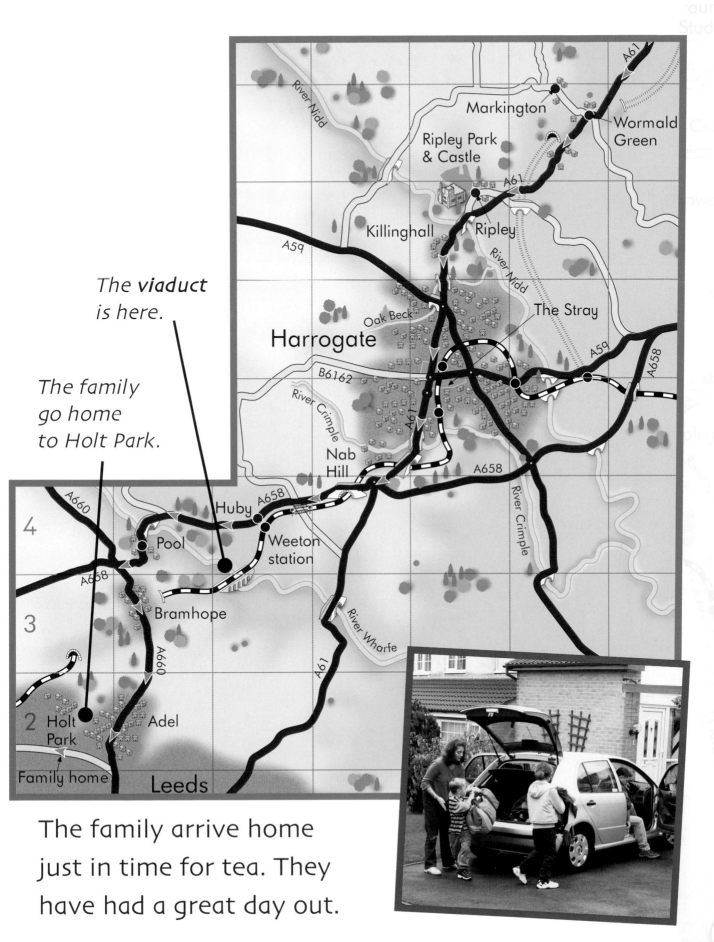

The *viaduct*
is here.

The family
go home
to Holt Park.

The family arrive home
just in time for tea. They
have had a great day out.

Follow the Map

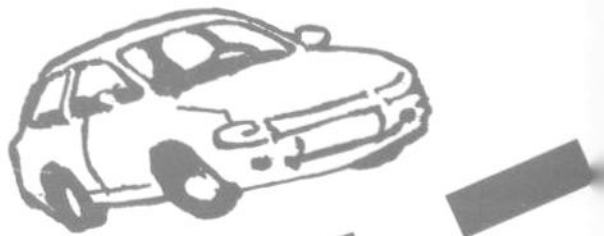

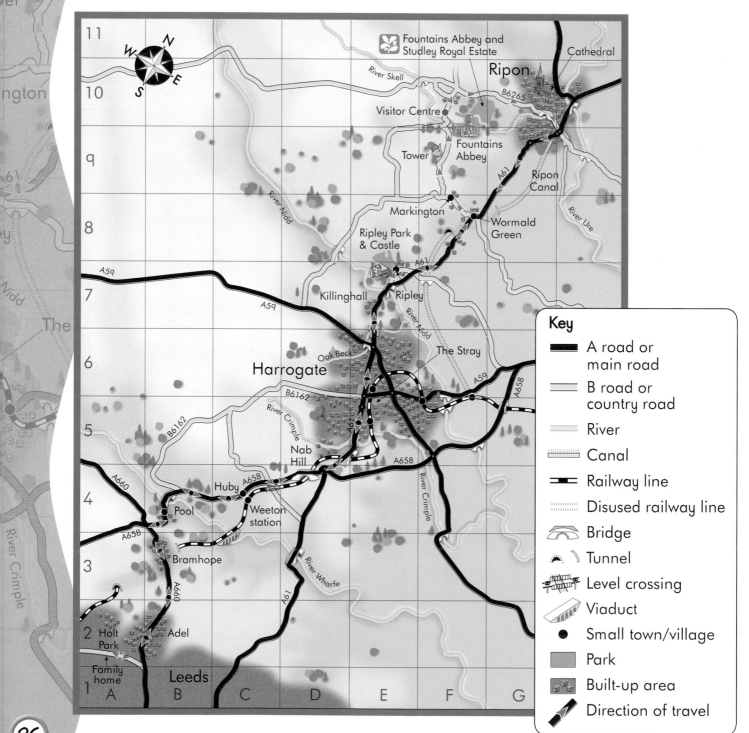

11
10
9
8
7
6
5
4
3
2
1
A
B
C
D
E
F
G
N
E
S
W
Fountains Abbey and
Studley Royal Estate
Cathedral
Ripon
River Skell
B6265
Visitor Centre
Fountains
Abbey
Tower
A61
Ripon
Canal
River Nidd
Markington
Wormald
Green
River Ure
Ripley Park
& Castle
A59
A61
Killinghall
Ripley
River Nidd
A59
Oak Beck
The Stray
Harrogate
A59
A658
B6162
River Crimple
B6162
A61
Nab
Hill
A658
A660
Huby
A658
Pool
Weeton
station
River Crimple
A658
Bramhope
River Wharfe
A660
A61
Holt
Park
Adel
Family
home
Leeds
Key
A road or
main road
B road or
country road
River
Canal
Railway line
Disused railway line
Bridge
Tunnel
Level crossing
Viaduct
Small town/village
Park
Built-up area
Direction of travel

Look again at the route the family took. They drove out of the city, passing through villages and towns. They crossed rivers and railway tracks, travelling along A roads and country roads. Have you ever been on a car journey like this? Find where the photographs were taken on the map.

1 Leaving home.

2 Joining the A658.

3 A level crossing near Huby.

4 Central Harrogate.

5 Bridge over the River Nidd.

6 Just past Markington.

7 At Fountains Abbey.

8 River Wharfe viaduct.

Activities

Work it Out

1. Look at pages 10 and 24. How does the railway line cross roads and rivers?

2. Look at pages 16 and 17. Why doesn't the main road (the A61) pass through the centre of the village of Ripley?

3. Look at page 19. What different methods do the family use to find their way to Fountains Abbey?

4. Look at the whole map on page 26. Can you find any other ways to get to Fountains Abbey? Why do you think the family chose the route they did?

Play a Game

- Look at the map on page 26. Adel, for example, is at grid reference B2.

- Write down five places that are in different squares. Challenge a friend to find their grid references.

- Give your friend the grid references for five other places. How long does it take your friend to find them on the map?

Glossary

cathedral
A big, important church.

city
A large town where lots of people live. Also, a place with a cathedral.

county
Britain is divided into large areas of land called counties. Yorkshire is a county in the north of England.

crossroads
The point where different roads meet.

direction
The way you go to get to where you want to be.

disused railway line
A stretch of railway that is no longer being used.

junction
The point where different roads meet.

landmark
Something that is easy to see in the distance.

level crossing
The point where a road crosses a railway line at ground level.

millstone
A circular stone used for grinding corn.

plan
A map of a place.

road map
A map used by people travelling between villages, towns and cities.

roundabout
A road junction where the traffic has to go round in a circle.

route
The way you chose to go to get from one place to another.

scale
The size used to show an area of land on a map, compared to the size of that land in real life. Large-scale maps show more detail than small-scale maps.

street map
A map that shows all the roads in a town or city.

town
A place with lots of roads and buildings, where many people live.

viaduct
A long bridge that takes a railway, road or canal over a valley.

village
A small group of houses and other buildings in the countryside.

Index

About this Book

FOLLOW THE MAP is designed as a first introduction to map skills. The series is made up of familiar journeys that the young reader is encouraged to follow. In doing so the child will begin to develop an understanding of the relation between maps and the geographical environment they describe. Here are some suggestions to gain the maximum benefit from CAR JOURNEY.

In this book, the reader is introduced to some basic geographical concepts, such as the compass directions north, south, east and west. This should provide a basis for further discussion, in relation to real journeys that the child has made.

A selection of different types of maps are illustrated in the book. It is helpful to expose the young reader to a wide variety of geographical resources. Build up a collection of maps of the child's local area, and discuss their different purposes.

On page 12 and 13, the reader can see two maps drawn to different scales. Discuss which map shows more detail and is therefore on a larger scale. The subject of scale can be a difficult one for young children to grasp, but these pages may provide a helpful starting point.

Look at page 16 and 17. Discuss the road layout on the map, and the reasons why the busy A61 bypasses the quiet village of Ripley. This may lead to further debate on the advantages and disadvantages of village bypasses. If possible, bring in local examples the child will be familiar with.

On page 19, the family use a landmark (an old tower) to help them work out where they are on the map. Talk together about local landmarks, and how they help people find their way about your neighbourhood.

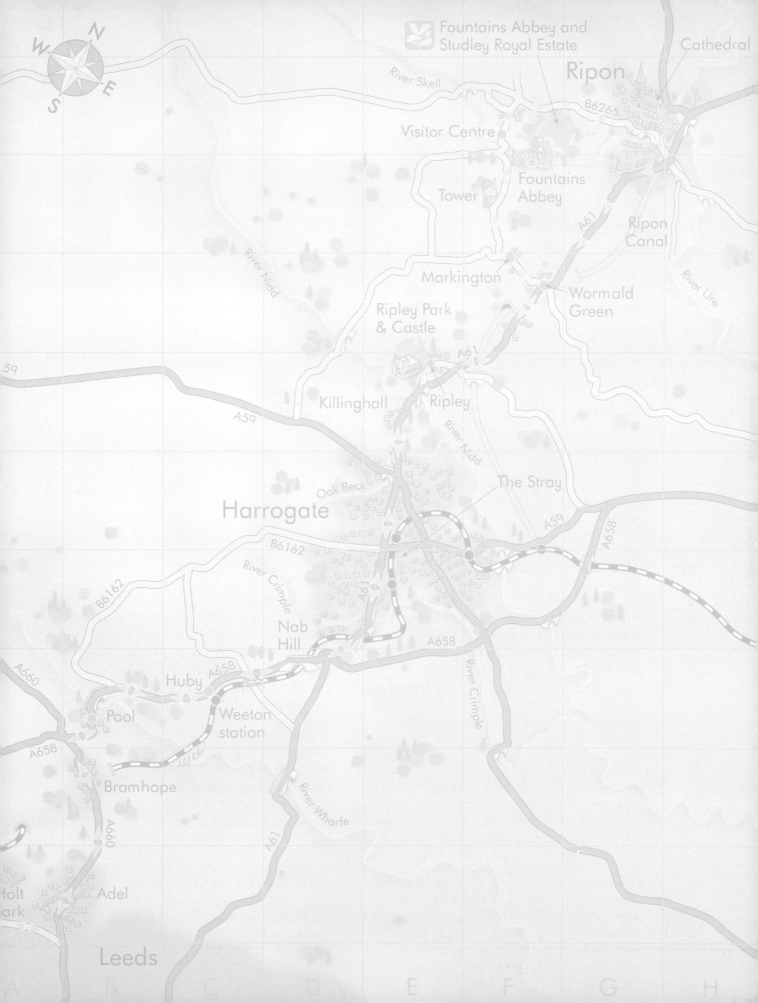